A Verseful of Jewish Holidays

Mazo Publishers
Jerusalem, Israel

Verseful Stories

Passover Prattle
Lag B'Omer
Ephraim Burns The Midnight Oil
The Dancing Dreidles
The Tu B'Shvat Trees
Queen Esther

A Verseful Of Jewish Holidays
Written by Ellen Gordon ~ Illustrated by Avi Katz

ISBN: 978-965-7344-47-7
Text Copyright © 2008 Ellen Gordon
Illustrations Copyright © 2008 Avi Katz

Published by
Mazo Publishers
Chaim Mazo, Publisher
P.O. Box 36084 ~ Jerusalem, Israel 91360

Web: www.mazopublishers.com ~ Email: cm@mazopublishers.com
USA: 1-815-301-3559 ~ Israel: 054-7294-565

Passover Prattle

In Egypt Jews were sad.
Their lives were very bad.
Their backs were whipped,
Their spirits clipped.
It made them very mad.

--Refrain--
Oh, Pharaoh, shame on you!
You troubled every Jew!
Despite your word,
Your shout was heard,
"I will not let them through!"

Young Moses' life was spared
Because his mother cared.
She hid him well
So none would tell.
With Pharaoh he was reared.

--Refrain--

And Moses quickly grew.
He cared for every Jew.
A man one day
Was hit and flayed.
The Egyptian Moses slew.

--Refrain--

Our Moses fled the scene,
But God did intervene.
He brought him home
To shake the throne
And spin his people's dream.

--Refrain--

Oh, Pharaoh wouldn't budge,
Though Moses pushed and nudged.
Ten plagues he got,
A sorry lot!
It left him with a grudge.

--Refrain--

Good Moses with his staff
Did split the sea in half.
The Jews then fled,
Away they sped,
Incurring Pharaoh's wrath.

--Refrain--

Then Pharaoh's men charged in,
Their horses in a spin.
The sea closed in,
They could not win.
They perished in the din.

--Refrain--

And with the utmost speed,
The Jews, at last, were freed.
Triumphant now
As Jews know how.
The world may well take heed!

Oh, Pharaoh, shame on you!
You troubled every Jew,
But though you tried
To keep your pride,
You had to let them through!

Lag B'Omer

For weeks the kids set out to comb the town,
they gathered every twig and log they found.
They hid their secret cache, reserved their space,
then Lag B'Omer night they took their place.

The fire burned away throughout the night.
The merging of the smoke, a thrilling sight.
The smell of burning wood was everywhere,
and roasting meat came wafting through the air.

The sounds of all their laughter filtered through
amidst their singing, strumming, humming, too.
Their gear and blankets strewn in random art,
a joyous time, delight to every heart.

Ephraim Burns The Midnight Oil

Ephraim was the youngest in his class.
The shortest, he would fumble every pass.
He sadly watched the others running fast.
In races he would always come in last.
"If only I could win just once, alas!"

His mother tried to lift his spirits high.
She told him he would grow as time flew by.
"You simply have to bide away your time
and learn to work on things where you feel prime.
You'll see ~ you'll soon be better by and by."

Ephraim wasn't satisfied with this.
He needed to excel, his greatest wish.
Impatience was the hallmark that was his.
"Why can't I show them all, that I can't miss.
To be ahead of others is my dish."

Ephraim had to show that he was tough.
He knew that he was made of sterner stuff,
but all the boys would do, was tease and bluff,
annoying just to see them acting gruff.
"It makes me very mad," he huffed and puffed.

Ephraim thought and thought ~
"What can I do,
to prove that I'm as good and better, too?
There must be something great to see me through
to demonstrate to them, a thing or two."

He pondered all the day ~ By night he knew!

"Shavuot's on the way, in three more days.
I'll stay awake all night. I will amaze.
They'll watch me learn. I'll earn their worthy praise.
Then they will see I'm not a boy who plays.
They'll say, 'He's like a man ~ alert he stays'."

Excited now, he scarce could eat or speak.
With this and everything, his knees felt weak.
"Shavuot's coming soon, in half a week,
they'll know at once I'm great, not small and meek.
I'll look them in the eye, no need to sneak."

And then it came, the long-awaited night.
His face was glowing, what a lovely sight!

"Oh, now they'll find I am a boy of might.
My power's strong, no weakling, short or slight,
but, rather, one who stays up all the night."

The synagogue had classes all night long.
This group of boys was stationed in the throng.
So proud they were,
their hearts were filled with song.
All learning, they could do no kind of wrong.
They felt alive. Indeed they did belong.

At ten o'clock their eyes were bright and clear.
Convinced they were that all would persevere.
Then Eli whispered loud in Chaim's ear,
"Ephraim, I am sure, will disappear.
By midnight, he'll be far away from here!"

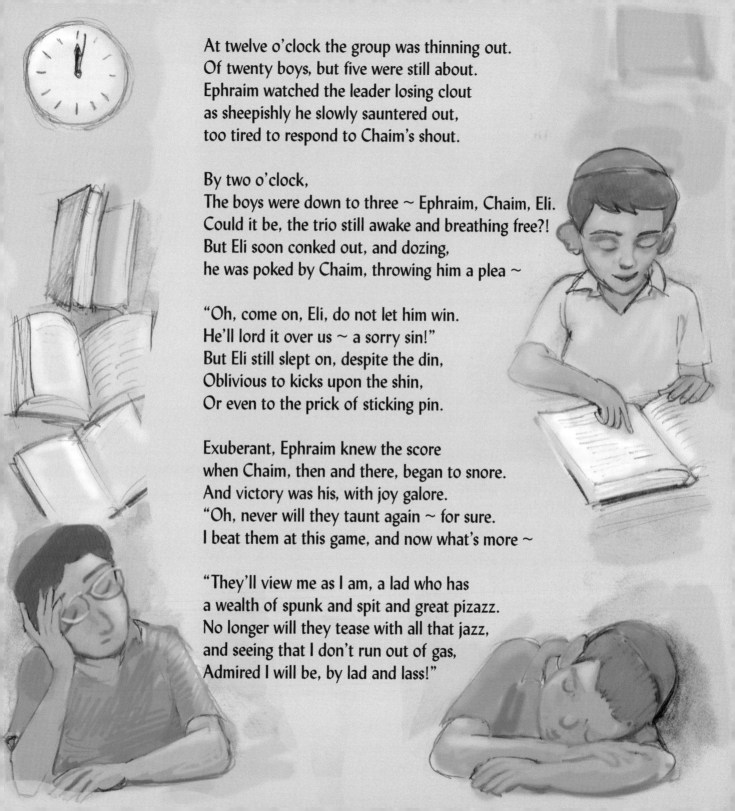

At twelve o'clock the group was thinning out.
Of twenty boys, but five were still about.
Ephraim watched the leader losing clout
as sheepishly he slowly sauntered out,
too tired to respond to Chaim's shout.

By two o'clock,
The boys were down to three ~ Ephraim, Chaim, Eli.
Could it be, the trio still awake and breathing free?!
But Eli soon conked out, and dozing,
he was poked by Chaim, throwing him a plea ~

"Oh, come on, Eli, do not let him win.
He'll lord it over us ~ a sorry sin!"
But Eli still slept on, despite the din,
Oblivious to kicks upon the shin,
Or even to the prick of sticking pin.

Exuberant, Ephraim knew the score
when Chaim, then and there, began to snore.
And victory was his, with joy galore.
"Oh, never will they taunt again ~ for sure.
I beat them at this game, and now what's more ~

"They'll view me as I am, a lad who has
a wealth of spunk and spit and great pizazz.
No longer will they tease with all that jazz,
and seeing that I don't run out of gas,
Admired I will be, by lad and lass!"

The Dancing Dreidels

Now gather round and listen.

It happened late at night.
The candles still were burning.
They made a lovely sight.

The pancakes, all were eaten ~
no food left, not a bite.

The children now were sleeping.
The house was locked and still,
when suddenly the dreidels
began a tripping trill.

The leader blew his whistle.
They marched around in drill,
and then they started spinning.
They twisted left and right.
The living room was shaking,
a noisy, crazy plight.

The furniture, astonished,
looked on with query gaze.
Then they, too, started dancing,
a sight that would amaze.

The sofa took to prancing.
He hopped and skipped about,
then somersaulted briskly.
He tumbled in and out.

The armchair watched the doings.
He would not be outdone,
and mustering his courage,
he quickly joined the fun.
He grabbed the old recliner
and led him in a jig,
and while the two were swinging
the lampshade lost her wig.

The windows gave a rattle.
The bookshelves dropped their books.
The table shook and wiggled,
while sending winsome looks.

The tumult reached the kitchen.
The dishes pitched and tossed.
The cups all took a tumble.
They fell, a few got lost.

And still the sleeping household
lay snuggled as they dozed.
They did not see the bedlam,
their eyelids, tight and closed.

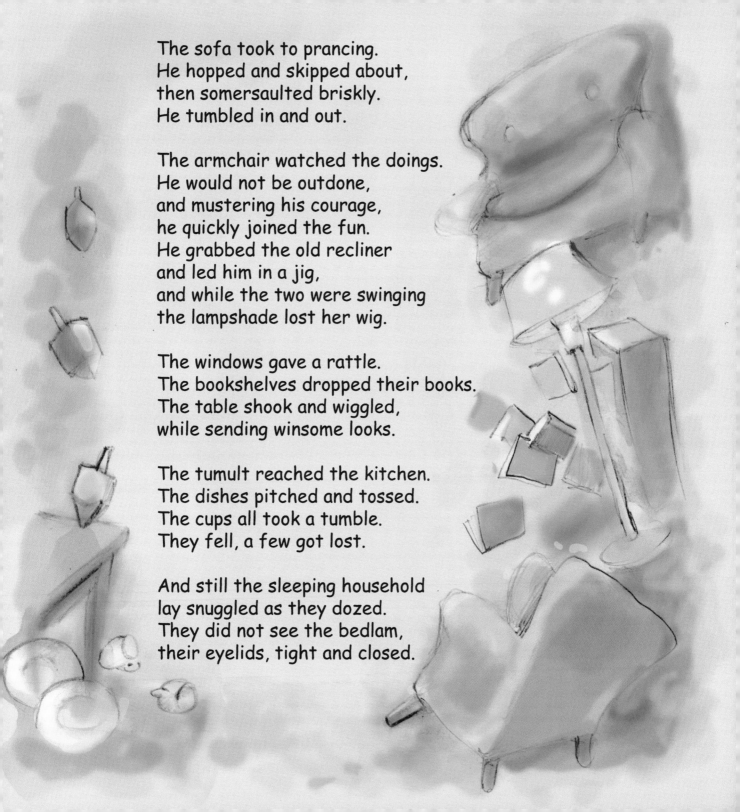

They heard not the commotion.
They missed the maddened stir
as pots and pans, together,
began their frantic whirl.

And causing much excitement,
the knives and forks woke up.
They shook the spoons and ladles.

The kitchenware jumped up,
upsetting all the garbage
with naughty, twinkling gleam.

The fridge then burst wide open
and spilled out all the cream.
It sent the plopping ice cubes
a-crashing to the floor,
along with dripping ice cream
a-melting on the door.

The din now reached the rafters,
the chimney caving in.

Then suddenly the furor
was silenced from within.

The children, from their bedrooms,
approached the winding stair
as dreidels, pots, and dishes
all scurried back to where
they'd started out their evening
in proper circumstance.

They faced the greeting children,
quite innocent their stance.

The sofa now was resting,
no evidence of fray,
the kitchen, clean and sparkling,
no sign of creamy spray.

The leader of the dreidels
put down his whistle bell.
He fell asleep, repentant,
too tired, if truth we tell!

The Tu B'Shvat Trees

I have to tell you what occurred
the day the forest overheard
that soon the men were coming down
to clear their home, to build a town.

The trees began a rustling sound.
They massed together, huddled round.
The leaves were fluttering about.
They'd start a protest, yell and shout.

But then the Oak Tree, strong and proud,
stood up and lectured, firm and loud ~

"We'll choose a spokesman, prove our case ~
unlawful to upset our race,
to bring in trucks, invade our space,
uprooting us without a trace!"

And all unanimous, they cried,
"Oh, Oak Tree, speak for us with pride.
Please tell them we've a right to live.
We have a world of things to give."

And Oak agreed to take their part.
He'd do his best with all his heart.
"I pray to God your faith I'll earn.
I'll do my utmost, make them learn
that man cannot survive alone.
He needs the wealth that we all own."

Then off he went and found the men
in conference call with planning pen,
prepared to send the wrecking crew
to raze the forest through and through.

And with the wisdom born of age,
he breathed in deep, contained his rage
and then began his strong appeal
to stir their conscience, make them feel
the justice of their noble cause.

The trees had much to give them pause,
so many things that they could share
and man could nurture with his care.

"Oh, lofty men, we see your need
to build your homes, a worthwhile deed,
but we've so much to give to you
and you to us, a favored two."

The man, however, hard and strained,
unsympathetic he remained.

"Our population's growing fast.
You are but trees, not of our class.
We must expand. It's good for us.
We can't contend with all this fuss."

But Oak would not be turned aside.
He stood his ground and kept his stride.

"If you but come to see our site,
you'll be enriched, you'll know our plight."

The man, at last, agreed to come.
There was a chance he would succumb
to all the trees could offer now.
Perhaps they would forestall the plow.
The man accompanied the Oak.
The two arrived. They hardly spoke.

Then Oak began his moving plea.
He wanted so the man to see
the beauty of the sprawling scene,
the woods so fresh, the air so clean.

"Come look at all that we have here, a world
of peace where dreams appear, and quiet
reigns and stirs the heart.
With hope restored, refreshed we start.
Each morning we perceive anew
the glory of the world renewed, reflected
in our thoughts sublime and in our
cherished land divine."

The man perceived the quiet glance
of Forest's graceful circumstance,
the magic aura of the trees in backdrop of
eternity, a scape removed from worried care,
where friendship grows and love is shared.

He viewed the Oak and Maple tree,
the Willow, Reed, and Shrubbery,
the Dogwood tree, majestic Pine,
each shrub and bush and gentle vine.

He watched the birds in artful flight.
He heard their chirp ~ to his delight.
At last he spoke with stirring words.

The trees, attentive, this they heard,

"I've seen your lovely paradise,
a world enthroned in rich surprise,
with thrilling sounds, enchanting sights.

The people's lives would all be blessed
if they were shown this peaceful rest,
away from hassle and from rush,
amidst the beauty and the plush
of forest green and azure blue,
the spectral scan of Nature's hue.

Their bustling days would intertwine
with healthy jaunts through lavish vine,
and work and play would intersperse
as somber mood gave way to verse,
inspired by idyllic scene of dawn and
sunset most pristine.

With picnic baskets, loving strolls,
a life enriched by nobler goals.
We'll build our township full of pride.
We'll jointly flourish,

Side By Side."

Queen Esther

Ilana, as a little girl, would weave a wealth of dreams.
She'd see herself in distant lands,
she'd shape her plans and schemes.
While other girls would play with dolls
and skip and jump and run,
she'd read, instead, her treasured tales ~
another kind of fun!

Imagining all sorts of things,
she'd curl up with a book,
oblivious to all around,
complete with starry look.

"Ilana, come, it's time to eat," her mother begged and cried.
Ilana, though, remembered not, no matter how she tried.

Her friends would come to plead with her.
They used a coaxing tone.
They soon despaired from calling her.
They left her on her own.

Her father tempted her with treats.
Her brother pulled and teased.
Her sister raised her hands and sighed,
"Ilana, won't you, please!"

In school the teacher called her name.
"Ilana, do wake up. Come join the class and
share your thoughts."

The teacher just gave up.

And then one day a thing occurred which
changed the tide for good.

The school announced the Purim play ~ at last
Ilana would put down her precious reading
book and notice those around.

The day the parts were handed out,
Queen Esther soon was found.
Ilana, in the starring role,
was perfect for the part.
They'd use her dreamy qualities.
She couldn't wait to start.

She felt alive, ebullient now!
She'd activate her plans.
Instead of just imagining,
she'd live her distant lands.

She'd visit Shushan royally,
and wear exotic dress.
She'd walk about with dignity.
She'd show all she possessed.

At home her parents watched her change,
enjoying every meal.
Her appetite was whetted now.
Her day was filled with zeal.

"Please, pass the butter, fill my cup.
I'm hungry as can be.
I need to build my energy.
Queen Esther, that is me!"

Enthusiastic, now she was.
In class she soon excelled.
Her happiness extended to
her friends who wished her well.
"Ilana, won't you play with us
and share your thrilling yarns?!"
Ilana now obliged them all,
displaying all her charms.

Rehearsals were a highlight to
her bustling, busy days.
With drama in her life, she now
began a brand new phase.
Her reading proved a boon to her,
enhancing all her skills.
The stage became a backdrop to
her fine artistic frills.

Ilana brought new meaning to
Queen Esther in her role.
It showed her sensitivity,
her special kind of soul.

Remembering a book she'd read,
she'd strut about and prance,
"King Ahashveros, do be kind
and give me just a glance."

The night of the performance saw
Ilana at her best.
The audience, with breath intake,
affirmed she'd passed the test.
They witnessed how she held herself
in regal, courtly grace,
and spellbound, they experienced
Queen Esther ~ face to face.

Ilana truly lived her part in thought,
and act, and deed.
She felt herself in Persia then,
compelled to see Jews freed.

And Haman was her enemy
and Mordechai her aide.

Together they allied themselves,
united, unafraid.

"Good people, come and rally round,
let's give a show of force.
Let's quash the tyrant, break his might,
begin a brave new course."

And victory was theirs to share,
with Jews in warm accord.
No longer would a foe arise
who dared to raise his sword.

Too soon the final curtain call, and then a latent pause ~
when suddenly the audience began a wild applause.

Ilana, of the story book, who'd plan and hope and
scheme, stepped out to bask in warm regard ~
and realized her dream!

Printed in the United States
113651LV00004B